"Every December we spi̇̇n̄——————————————————————...............
rightly calls our 'shop-till-you-drop, make-sure-everybody-is-
totally-happy, gift-buying, food-gorging panic attack' called
Christmas. If, like me, you're exhausted already, then *An Even
Better Christmas* is for you. This book guides us all into real
'peace on earth,' starting way down deep in our hearts."

**RAY ORTLUND, Pastor, Immanuel Church, Nashville;
President, Renewal Ministries**

"In *An Even Better Christmas*, Matt Chandler asks a life-changing
question: in the Christmas story, are we less like the wise men
and more like the religious leaders, who knew *about* God's King
but didn't want to know him? Once that question is in your
mind, your Christmases will never be the same again. I'm so
grateful to Matt for raising it, and it has made me much more
excited about Christmas this year."

**RICO TICE, Founder, Christianity Explored Ministries;
Author, *Capturing God* and *A Very Different Christmas***

"At Christmas we celebrate God's intervention in world history.
The shepherds and wise men were smart enough to check it
out. Matt Chandler, who faced a head-on collision with life-
threatening cancer, is so glad that *he* checked it out. Let me
encourage you to read Matt's amazing story and check out the
Christ of Christmas for yourself. God wants to intervene in
your life too."

**TERRY VIRGO, Founder, Newfrontiers;
Author, *Life Tastes Better***

MATT CHANDLER

AN EVEN

Better

CHRISTMAS

the**good**book
COMPANY

An Even Better Christmas
© The Village Church 2018

Published by
The Good Book Company

Websites
North America: www.thegoodbook.com
UK & Europe: www.thegoodbook.co.uk
Australia: www.thegoodbook.com.au
New Zealand: www.thegoodbook.co.nz

ISBN: 9781784982881 | Printed in India

Design by André Parker

Contents

Something Better

I've always loved Christmas. But when I was growing up, there were rules.

The essential rules in the Chandler home were basically:

- You don't steal.
- You don't kill.
- You don't do drugs.
- And you don't decorate for Christmas until after Thanksgiving.

My wife, Lauren, isn't wired that way. She would start celebrating Christmas in January if I wasn't such a bastion of "not until after Thanksgiving."

But once we get past that last Thursday of November, I've always been all in. Near my house, there's a street

MATT CHANDLER

that every year decorates their neighborhood with
Disney characters and Christmas lights. Around 500
times in the run-up to Christmas, my youngest daughter
will ask us on the way home to turn down that street so
she can see them... and about 412 of those requests
I'm going to say yes to, and we're just going to go down
there and watch it.

If that doesn't prove my commitment to Christmas, I'll
let you know that my family watches *Elf* every year. And
by watch, I mean we watch it about a thousand times
together. It's a tradition in the Chandler household that
early in December, there's a conversation in my house
that goes something like this:

Kids: "What are we going to do tonight?"

Me: "I don't know."

Kids: "We could watch *Elf*?"

Me: "It's after Thanksgiving. Let's go."

I love Christmas. In fact, I love it more now than
when I was a kid. And I've even relaxed the "not
until Thanksgiving" rule (I'll tell you why in the last
chapter, and that can be your reward for reading
between here and there). But please don't misunder-
stand me. Christmas at the Chandlers isn't always—
isn't ever—perfect. Far from it. As much as I love the
holiday, there is a vast gap between the Christmas that

the commercials promise and the Christmas that we experience as a family.

After all, there is no holiday in the Western world that suffers more propaganda than this season. Every commercial, every special TV show, everything we see lays before us this great promise that this is the year it's all going to come together.

This year, we'll gather with our families and a Christmas miracle is going to take place. Strife will dissipate, and tension will melt, and annoyance will disappear, and all the sorrow of the last year will give way to cheerful joy.

This year, your kids are going to be great. They're going to open up their presents and be like, "Thank you, Mother. This is perfect," and they're not going to get bored within five hours (or minutes) of opening them. Not this year.

That's what the commercials tell you.

And I want to tell you it's not going to happen. Those commercials are over-promising. And, in fact, they are under-promising.

See, I love Christmas—but it's not because I've been kidded by the commercials that at Christmas everything might be perfect. I love Christmas because it's the start of the story that means one day (not this Christmas, but one day) everything will really be perfect.

So in this little book, I simply want to offer you something better than those commercials do—not just for this season but for every day and month of your life. I want to lay before you something that will stay long after the tree is gone (either dead gone or back-up-in-the-attic gone)—something that will still be there after the carols have faded and the lights have been put away.

I want to show you, whoever you are and whatever is going on in your life as you sit down to read this (and thanks for taking the time to read this), how the first Christmas can meet you where you are and provide you with hope where you are.

This is the season of massive shop-till-you-drop, make-sure-everybody-is-totally-happy, gift-buying, food-gorging panic attack. And in the midst of all that, I want to lead you through some things that the Christmas story tells us are true about God—to help you to stop… and breathe… and refocus your heart… and see who God is, what he's like, what he's up to. I want you to have an even better Christmas than the commercials offer, by celebrating not only that Christ has come but also that his power is at work in the present day, and that he will return on one future day—this time not as a baby but as a ruling, restoring King.

Christmas is about more than saying, "Oh, isn't it great that six-pound baby Jesus was born into the world?"

That's a piece of what Christians celebrate, but it's only a piece.

I'd like to introduce you to—or remind you of—the God who gets involved… who gives joy… and who is worth your trust.

Whether or not your house obeys the "not until after Thanksgiving" rule, you can enjoy the God we discover in Christmas through December, and out into January, all year round, and on and on.

God Gets Involved

I'll never forget the experience of having our first child, Audrey. It's not that the second and third, Reid and Norah, weren't important. There's just something unique about your first. The joy, the excitement, and—especially—the preparation.

I'm pretty sure we almost went broke buying heaps of things we did and didn't need for this little life. We spent so many hours just talking and thinking about what she would be like. And by the time Audrey arrived in this world, we were prepared for everything—well, everything except how to parent a child.

The first Christmas was the culmination of a lot of preparation, and I'm not just talking about what it was probably like for Mary to prepare to have her first child. The birth that lies at the heart of this story was thousands of years in the planning. The whole of the Old Testament part of the Bible—about two-thirds of the books that make up the Bible—detail the preparations that went into the first Christmas. It's full of glimpses of the shape of what would happen. We're jumping into one of those glimpses, 1,400 years before Mary's child was born.

WELCOME TO THE MESS

In 1400 BC the Israelites found themselves living in a foreign empire, oppressed into slavery by the ruler of that superpower, the Pharaoh of Egypt. There's nothing strange about any of that, of course— tragically, oppression and slavery are part of every era of human history. But the real kicker for the Israelites was that they had been promised centuries before by the God of the Bible that, as his chosen people, they would be loved, helped, and blessed by him, and that through them somehow one day the whole world would be loved, helped, and blessed by him.

Yet here they were, slaves in a foreign land, and here's what the Bible tells us life was like for them:

> [The Egyptians] set taskmasters over them to afflict them with heavy burdens. They built for Pharaoh store cities, Pithom and Raamses.
>
> (Exodus chapter 1, verse 11)

And then it got worse.

In an effort to prevent his slaves from rising up against him, Pharaoh decided to get rid of all the baby boys born to the Israelites: he "commanded all his people, 'Every son that is born to the Hebrews you shall cast into the [River] Nile'" (Exodus 1 v 22).

They're struggling. They're afflicted. They're seeing no future. That may resonate with your heart right now. Maybe you've been walking through something as oppressive or unjust or upsetting as what those Israelites faced. Maybe it's not been as stark, but your struggle is no less real. There are those of us this Christmas season who are quietly thinking, "Yes, I do feel oppressed and trapped, and I'm losing hope." Maybe it's because of people. Maybe it's because of a sense of darkness. Maybe it's because of your own regrets or flaws. Maybe it's just because of the gap between how you thought life would turn out and how life is.

This is why I want to start this book about Christmas here, centuries before the famous events of the nativity story (don't worry—we will get to the shepherds and the wise men soon enough); because this was a time when the world was clearly in a mess, and when God's people were truly struggling. It must have felt to the Israelites right then as if they had been abandoned by their God—that God was nowhere to be found and that his promises were make-believe. And let's face it, even at Christmas, the truth is that our world is a mess;

and if you and I are being honest, we're a mess, too. If you're like me, I'm betting that the year just gone held some pain for you, some sadness, and some frustration, as well as some joys and successes. And you're bringing all that into your Christmas.

So, the question is: is there a God out there who really cares, and who can actually help?

AND GOD...

As the story of the Israelites in Egypt goes on, we see these words:

> *The people of Israel groaned because of their slavery and cried out for help. Their cry for rescue from slavery came up to God. And God heard their groaning… (Exodus 1 v 23-24)*

That's a profound truth that I want to lay before you. God knew. God knows. Regardless of what you're walking in, God is not a stranger to where you are. God is not ignorant of what's going on in your heart, in your life, in your mind, in your relationships. He is not surprised, not shocked, not shuddering, not wondering what to do. God hears you. God knows you.

And God intervenes. We know this because the way in which God intervenes is so spectacular that they keep making movies about it, though I'm not sure there can ever be a better Moses than Charlton Heston.

Moses was born an Israelite baby and faced death at the hands of a murderous king. His mom tried to keep him away from danger by putting him in a basket and floating him down the Nile (the river he was due to be drowned in). There (in the definition of irony) Moses was found by Pharaoh's daughter, picked up, and brought up by her in the palace of the man who wanted to kill him.

So Moses is raised among the elite of Egypt, until one day he sees that a fellow Israelite is being dealt with harshly by an Egyptian guard and Moses ends up killing that guard. (The Bible is not a fairy story, because it's about reality—it's grimy.) Moses hides the body and hopes he's got away with it. But people find out, and then Pharaoh finds out, causing Moses to flee to the mountains and become a shepherd.

Yet God starts to turn things around. He appears to Moses through a bush that is burning but not being burned up and says, *I've heard the cries of my people. I'm going to deliver them. You're going to go speak to Pharaoh for me.*

Moses says, *I stutter.*

God says, *I don't.*

Moses goes on to make more excuses (as if arguing with the God of the universe will get you very far), and God intervenes at every excuse. He tells Moses, *You are weak and frail, I know. I'm not. I'm going with you.*

Let's go. (By the way, that's all paraphrased, if you didn't pick up on it.)

Moses goes back to Egypt, and a confrontation between Pharaoh and God ensues (guess who wins?). Pharaoh is confident, because he thinks he's divine too, and that he's more powerful than this God of the Israelites, whose people are simply slaves. So God intervenes again and again. Through his servant Moses, he turns the water in Egypt into blood. He covers the land with frogs. Then gnats. Then flies. Then the livestock begins to die. Then the people break out in boils. Then hail comes down. Then locusts raid. Then one day, it just stops being day. It's dark. All the time. And finally life itself starts to be withdrawn by God. In each intervention, God is proving that he is real, and he is all-powerful, and he does have complete control over the world and every atom in it.

And Pharaoh goes back and forth: *No, I don't need to listen to God. Oh, OK, I'm listening. Actually, no, I won't—I'm digging my heels in.* Even when he finally lets the Israelites go, he sends his army to get them back (so God uses the Red Sea to protect his people and defeat Pharaoh's forces).

Now it's easy to judge Pharaoh (honestly, I think seeing every drop of water turn to blood would've been enough for me)—but then again, think of how often we dig in our heels against God: how often we're confident that we know more than him—that we know best. When you think about it that way, we're as much like Pharaoh in this story as we are Moses or the Israelites.

YOU REALLY EXPECT ME TO BELIEVE THIS?

Maybe you're thinking at this point:

All right, Chandler. I liked "God knows." I liked the thought that there is a God who hears. That's good. But you're losing me on "God intervenes," because let me tell you, in my life, in the kind of brokenness I'm walking in—in the frustration, the anger, the anxiety—this kind of divine, miraculous intervention is nowhere to be found. There has been no water turned to blood in my world. This miraculous God you speak of has not intervened in my life. Do you really expect me to believe or trust in a God who rules over all when I can't see him doing anything at all, anywhere?!

And maybe you want to add:

And it's not like I haven't been trying. I've even been going to church. But I'm still anxious. My life and my relationships are still on fire. That God in the book of Exodus—why doesn't he show up now?

To which I want to say,

But you are thinking this out, and you are reading this book. You're taking time out to read a book about God and you're thinking about him and you're wrestling with these things, and maybe that's all a great surprise to you. Might this not be God starting to intervene in your life?

(Don't put the book down just to prove your point!)

See, God started intervening for his people when he spoke to Moses in the mountains. At that point, his people had no idea he'd started to go to work for them. And as I look back on my own life, I can see lots of interventions of God that didn't seem much at the time, but turned out to make all the difference to me.

The first miracle took place during high school football when I ended up hanging out with a group of guys who were serious about Jesus. I was rude and offensive, yet they kept inviting me to hang out—kept inviting me along to listen to Christian things. They were kind and acted with integrity. I was foul-mouthed and pursuing women. They were wondering whether it was wise to watch *Terminator 2*. I'd already seen it four times. And I was finding life dissatisfying and wondering whether there was something better. God was intervening.

The second intervention was when I was in the football locker room (if you've not been in one of those, it is not a place of high-level intellectual discourse—there's a lot of lying going on and a lot of the lying is about women). But it was there that a guy named Jeff, in front of everybody, said to me, "I need to tell you about Jesus. When do you want me to do that?" God was intervening.

And, now that I have eyes to see it, I can see him intervening all the time. He knows me. He hears me. He intervenes for me.

Maybe you're so busy looking for water to turn into blood and waiting for plagues of flies and gnats—maybe you're so determined to demand some kind of "show me you're bending the laws of nature" type of intervention—that you've forgotten to look at the little miracles that are right in front of you even in this moment. You're in a society that increasingly doesn't take God seriously and prefers the promises of the commercials to the realities of the first Christmas, despite the fact that those promises are proved empty again and again—yet you are reading these words… doesn't it look like God is intervening in your life at some level?

1400 years before Christmas got started, God was showing that he knows, he hears, and he gets involved in the mess and the difficulties of this world. He doesn't just leave us where we are. He gets involved and he changes things. That's the God of the Bible.

WELCOME TO THE MAIN EVENT

Those were dark times in Egypt. And then God started to intervene. And that intervention began by him protecting a chosen baby, so that a murderous king wouldn't be able to get rid of him. Which may sound familiar…

After Jesus was born in Bethlehem of Judea in the days of Herod the king, behold, wise men from the east came to Jerusalem, saying, "Where is he who has been born king of the Jews?" … When Herod the king heard this, he was troubled…

[Once those wise men had traveled on to Bethlehem, found Jesus, and then left for their own country] an angel of the Lord appeared to Joseph in a dream and said, "Rise, take the child and his mother, and flee to Egypt, and remain there until I tell you, for Herod is about to search for the child, to destroy him." And he rose and took the child and his mother by night and departed to Egypt…

Then Herod, when he saw that he had been tricked by the wise men, became furious, and he sent and killed all the male children in Bethlehem and in all that region who were two years old or under.

(Matthew 2 v 1-2, 3, 13-14, 16)

(Even Christmas, which we've tidied up for kids' nativity plays, reminds us that the Bible is not a fairy story; it's grimy reality.)

Those were dark times in Judea, the land of the Jews—the descendants of the Israelites. Judea was part of the Roman Empire and under the oppression of the Romans' brutal puppet-king, Herod. And God began to intervene by protecting a chosen baby, so that a murderous king wouldn't be able to get rid of him.

What happened at Christmas is the beginning of another exodus story. It is God knowing that humanity and that life is not all we want it to be—not all he designed it to be. It is God responding to people crying out and asking for him to do something: to hold to his promises to love, help, and bless the people he's made. It's God getting involved by using another man whose very birth and survival was miraculous.

But this is bigger—and better. If the exodus story were the rehearsal, this was the main event. It's what all the preparations were leading toward. Because this time, God didn't choose to intervene through a man he'd raised up from among the people. This time, God intervened through becoming a man himself, by becoming one of his people.

So when his angel announced to Mary, a young, soon-to-be-married girl, that she was going to have a baby, he told her that this was no ordinary child:

You will conceive in your womb and bear a son, and you shall call his name Jesus. He will be great and will be called the Son of the Most High. (Luke 1 v 31-32)

AT THE BASE OF THE UNIVERSE

The angel's words take us deep into what the Bible says about who God is. The Bible rejects the idea of God as a distant force who created everything to show his power. Equally, it rejects the notion of warring deities, who, in their conflict, ended up making the universe as a kind of ground to fight out their struggles upon. The Bible shows us that God is a Trinity—a perfect community of One, in which there are three distinct, separate persons who are all fully God. (This is confusing to us—and that's fine. I mean, a God whose entire essence could be understood by our minds would be a pretty limited kind of God, right?) The Bible calls those three persons in this one God the Father (among other names, including "the Most High"), the Son, and the Holy Spirit.

This trinitarian God delights in the relationships within himself, and created everything so that he could enjoy relationship with the people he made. So the base of this universe is not power, or struggle, but gladness-filled, relational joy. That's why right-minded humans all through the ages have found their greatest satisfaction not in seizing power or in fighting each other but in enjoying relationships.

Now come back to that angel's words. The trinitarian God has existed since eternity—Father, Son, and Holy Spirit. And now Mary is going to be pregnant, through the work of the Holy Spirit, because the Father is sending his Son into the world that he made:

> *You shall call his name Jesus. He will be great and will be called the Son of the Most High. (Luke 1 v 31-32)*

This was no mere man. This baby was, as the Bible puts it…

> *"Immanuel" (which means, God with us).*
> *(Matthew 1 v 23)*

God with us. As a baby.

See, Christmas is not about pretending that everything is great and we don't struggle or suffer. Christmas is about acknowledging that sometimes things are not great and we do struggle and suffer, even at Christmas—and that God knows this, God hears us, and God has got involved for us. You live in a world that has been visited by its Maker. God showed up. God didn't send Moses. God came himself. That's how committed he is to your good. And when you see him that way and see this world that way, it changes how you walk through the hard times and how you celebrate Christmas.

Does God intervene?

Could God get involved in your life?

Christmas says, *Yes. He already did.*

God Brings Joy

Who did God come for? It's probably not who you'd think.

Remember how God marked his getting involved in the Israelites' lives? He pitched up and spoke to a shepherd — to Moses. Well, the same thing happened at Christmas— God spoke to a group of shepherds to make the most world-changing announcement this world has seen.

Now, everyone knows that shepherds are a key part of the Christmas story. Many of us have memories of dressing up as kids in a sheet and towel (because that's exactly what first-century Middle-Eastern shepherds wore). So, when I tell you God sent an angel to appear to the shepherds, you just go, "Yes, I know." It's no surprise.

But it was at the time.

THE LEAST LIKELY PEOPLE

Shepherds were, in fact, the least likely people God would choose to include in what he was doing in his world.

In first-century Judea, shepherds were considered outsiders, on the edges of normal society. They were so mistrusted that their testimony was inadmissible evidence in a court of law. First-century Jews believed that God didn't like shepherds—and they didn't like them, either. The most pious of Jews would not buy milk, lambs, or wool from shepherds; they assumed it was stolen. The religious elite of that day saw them as unclean, filthy, unwanted, and outside of God's favor. A philosopher in Alexandria, one of the centers of the intellectual world at the time, went so far as to say, "There is no more disreputable an occupation than that of a shepherd."

Yet when "the time came for [Mary] to give birth [and] she gave birth to her firstborn son" in Bethlehem, "in the same region there were shepherds out in the field, keeping watch over their flock by night. And an angel of the Lord appeared to them, and the glory of the Lord shone around them" (Luke 2 v 6-9). And then those shepherds get a whole multitude of angelic visitors praising God in their field.

The time has come to announce the news that God's Son himself has been born as a baby—that God himself is visiting his world, that God's getting involved. Yet God does not choose to go to the moral, the upright, or the elite. He goes to the excluded, to the outsiders.

At one of the turning points of history, it's as if God calls an angel over and says, *Tell them.*

The angel is like, *Them?!*

Yeah, the shepherds.

Do you know what they're like? Don't you mean go tell the religious guys?

Yeah, I know what the shepherds are like, because I'm God. Go. Tell the shepherds.

What?

Go. Tell. The. Shepherds.

Err. OK.

And then a whole choir's worth of other angels come up…

Hey, can we go?

No, I'm giving this job to him.

Yeah, but we really want to be a part of this.

All right, fine. Go, but give him his moment first. You can show up late.

If I asked anyone in the first century to come up with a list of those God would announce the good news to first, not one person would put the shepherds on a top-100 list. But the angel was sent to the least likely people because God came for the least likely people. This event set a pattern for Jesus reaching out to surprising people all through his life: a pattern of him living on the margins, of him welcoming in those whom other people had written off. Again and again, Jesus got into trouble with the influencers and the self-proclaimed good people because he hung out with those who had been rejected, those who had messed up:

> *And as [Jesus] reclined at table in [a follower's] house, many tax collectors [hated because they were traitors] and sinners [those who didn't follow the accepted norms of the day] were reclining with Jesus and his disciples, for there were many who followed him. And the scribes of the Pharisees [the religious leaders], when they saw that he was eating with sinners and tax collectors, said to his disciples, "Why does he eat with tax collectors and sinners?"*

> *And when Jesus heard it, he said to them, "Those who are well have no need of a physician, but those who are sick. I came not to call the righteous, but sinners."*
> *(Mark 2 v 15-17)*

People who think they're good can't understand Jesus, just as someone who thinks they're completely healthy wouldn't understand why a doctor had decided to come visit them. People who know they're not good are ready to understand Jesus, just as someone who knows they're sick is ready to listen to a doctor. The message of Christmas is not: "Get your house tidy, get the food right, pretend that your family is like the Waltons. Then God will bless you." The message of Christmas is: "God knows you, he knows you need help, he knows you've wandered away, and he's come to you anyway."

Jesus came to save the "sick." You are never too bad for God. And you are never good enough for God. Jesus didn't come for those who think they're fine. Knowing this frees you to be honest about yourself without needing to crush yourself. There's great joy in living with both honesty and hope.

That's why the first people to hear that "Unto you is born this day in the city of David a Savior, who is Christ the Lord" were outsiders—not the elite. That's why the angel was sent to the shepherds. That's why it was they who received this privilege.

But privileged as their experience was, it was not an enjoyable one, at first:

An angel of the Lord appeared to them, and the glory of the Lord shone around them, and they were filled with great fear. (Luke 2 v 9)

The best way to translate that word "glory" is weight. In that field, the weight of God showed up. It's a kind of weight that is heavier than anything else. When the glory of God shows up, it reshapes and reorders. It pushes out and breaks free. There is nothing as weighty as this in the universe. When the glory of God shows up, it changes everything. When you get a glimpse of the God of Christmas, things happen.

ME, MY DAUGHTER, AND LEBRON JAMES

And the first thing that happens when you glimpse God is… you are "filled with great fear."

That's because when the glory of God shows up, it exposes us for who we are. The most consistent thing I've found in conversations about religion is that almost everybody thinks they're a good person. They really just have no concept of God ever being frustrated or upset with them at all.

Why is that? Because we tend to have a very small concept of God. We think he's a tame house-cat. But he isn't. He's a lion. That's what the shepherds understand when his weight shows up. It exposes them.

When we say we're good people, what we mean is that we're good people on a sliding scale. It's relative. If I play basketball with my youngest daughter, Norah, here is what I can say about myself. I am powerful. I am fast. I am strong. I am unstoppable. I am brilliant. I'll dunk all over. She is unable to stop it in any way. I am great.

Then the door opens, and LeBron James walks in. (If you are not a basketball fan, you should know he's the best basketball player since Michael Jordan, and if you don't know who Michael Jordan is, then he's well worth looking up on YouTube.)

Now, am I powerful? No.

Am I fast? No.

Strong? No.

Unstoppable? No.

Brilliant? No.

Just a second ago, I was great. All it took was LeBron to walk on court, and I slid down.

We think we're good because we compare ourselves to other people. We can always find aspects of our lives that look great, and we can always find people who do worse than us and make us feel better about ourselves.

Then the glory of God shows up.

Compare yourself to him. He's perfect. Powerful. Wise. Pure. Kind. Loving. Always. When the glory—the weight—of God shows up, we see ourselves as we are. Every bit of our swagger, every bit of our confidence, every bit of our self-justification melts in the light of his glory. When the King steps in the room, our confidence melts away.

Not only can we not compete; we can't even stay on court. You put me on court with an NBA team, and I can't say, "Hang on, give me a couple decades and I will get up to standard." It isn't going to happen. I can't say, "Well, when I play with Norah in our yard I look pretty good." It doesn't matter. You put me on that court, and either I will walk off in shame or the coach will take me off.

I can't co-exist with LeBron. And I definitely can't co-exist with the glory of God. And neither could those shepherds, which is why they were so terrified. I'm sure they weren't Bible experts—but, living in Israel, they would have known what tended to happen to people when the glory of God showed up.

They died.

Even Isaiah, one of the greatest of God's messengers or prophets, realized he could not co-exist with the glory of God when he caught just a glimpse of it: "Woe is me ... I am a man of unclean lips [and] my eyes have seen the King" (Isaiah 6 v 5). Even Peter, who would become one of the greatest of the early Christian leaders, said, "Depart from me, for I am a sinful man, O Lord" (Luke 5 v 8) when he first met Jesus and realized he was God visiting his world.

When we see the weight of God, we realize that we're not like him. It exposes those duplicitous secrets we think no one else knows. You have no secrets from God. There is no area of thought or life that God is not absolutely tuned into. Church attendance and good deeds don't dupe him into overlooking what's underneath. And so God's glory reveals to us the truth that we are, as the Bible would put it, sinners. We are not good people, deserving of heaven.

Here's why this matters more than anything else. Beyond death we will either enjoy the warmth of the presence of God in perfection, or we will be shut out of his glory, with nothing good. And because we all "fall short of the glory of God" (Romans 3 v 23), by rights we are all headed for a future outside his loving presence.

When the glory of God shows up, it exposes us for who we are—and that's terrifying. But that's not all the glory of God does. It also drives out that fear and replaces it with joy.

FEAR NOT

Look at what the angel says to those quaking shepherds:

> *Fear not, for behold, I bring you good news of great joy that will be for all the people. For unto you is born this day in the city of David a Savior, who is Christ the Lord. (Luke 2 v 10-11)*

Now, I love this. "Fear not..." Why? Because "I bring you..." What? "Good news." What is the good news that drives out the fears of our hearts about the unsur-vive-able glory of God? Well, John 3 v 17 is a great verse for you to hear, whether you've been a Christian for years or this is the first time you've thought about these things:

> God did not send his Son into the world to condemn the world, but in order that the world might be saved through him.

When Jesus Christ showed up, he was born as the life raft in a sea of condemnation, death, and destruction. He did not come to sink us, to condemn us—he came to rescue us. The good news is that God has made a way where we could not make a way for ourselves.

When we think about what we ourselves are like, most of us veer between two verdicts. Most of us spend most of our time assuming we're good—but then sometimes we worry that we're not. So we alternate between assuming God likes us and thinking that he doesn't.

Many people (both those who go to church and those who don't) instinctively feel that God should just love them and agree with them on everything. Deep down, they believe that God needs us to tell him how we can be happiest and what we most need in our lives. He should just go about sprinkling fairy dust and announcing, *Guys, you're great.*

Then other people (both those who go to church and those who don't) instinctively feel that God doesn't like them much—he's just waiting for us to trip up so he can slam us.

Back when I started going to church, I definitely was not a Christian and was really not sure what it was all about. And I remember thinking, "If there is a God, and he looks down and sees that I'm here, he's going to be frustrated and annoyed that I'm in his joint because I have not followed him and have my own ways of doing things. In fact, I've verbally mocked him for years. Now, all of a sudden, I'm sitting in his living room."

But the God of Christmas did not come to condemn me, or you. He came to rescue us. He did not come to read out a charge sheet of all your sin. He came to wipe your slate clean—to forgive your every sin past, present, and future. He's not the God who gives you a second chance and then tells you to do better this time round. He's the God who comes to give you a third chance and a fourth—to keep forgiving you. That's grace, and you can never out-sin the grace of God. Equally, you will always need it.

God did not come to tell you that he doesn't like you. He came to show you that he loves you. Which is why God's plan included not just the events of Christmas but the events of Easter.

LIVING AND DYING

It's weird, if you think about it, that the symbol of Christianity isn't a cradle, to celebrate all the glorious events of the first Christmas.

It's even weirder that instead of a cradle, it's a cross— an instrument of death and shame, designed by the Romans to kill people in the most brutal way imaginable. Christians are basically choosing to put the ancient equivalent of an electric chair on chains around our necks and on the sides of the buildings where we meet together. If the sight of a cross has lost its impact on you, then maybe you've grown too accustomed to seeing it.

So why a cross? Because God's Son did not come to this world primarily to live in it, but to die for it. The cross where Jesus Christ died was the place where he took our sin and bore its weight, its penalty—separation from his Father's glory. On the cross, Jesus stepped outside of God's glorious presence and died for all those things that stop us stepping into it. There, he took what should most terrify us—the experience of being shut out of God's presence. And so there, he can offer what we most need—God's delight in us and God's welcome of us. God is gloriously perfect, and he won't have imperfection anywhere near him. So the perfect human took humanity's imperfections so that he could offer men and women his own perfection.

This is how God made a way for us to walk into his glory beyond death and enjoy it, and bask in it, and love it. This is why Christians love to talk about the death of Jesus even more than we love to talk about the birth of Jesus. God did not send his Son at Christmas to condemn us—he sent his Son at Christmas so that at Easter he could save us.

That's the point of Christmas. If you accept Jesus' offer of rescue and forgiveness, you need no longer fear being exposed by God when one day you stand before his glory. Instead, you can know "great joy," because you are exposed but you're also forgiven. What a gift! You know God knows everything about you, and that he loves you anyway. What a gift! You know that he came as Jesus to bring you into an eternal future of enjoying his glory, rather than being shut out of it.

The glory of God, when you see it at the first Christmas and see it at the first Easter, drives out fear and replaces it with joy.

ORDINARY TUESDAYS

And that changes every day. Not just your Christmas Day, but your normal, ordinary, Tuesdays in the middle of May. That's what happened to the shepherds.

When the angel told them to go see God, the Lord, whom they would find as "a baby wrapped in swaddling cloths and lying in a manger," *they did:*

The shepherds said to one another, "Let us go over to Bethlehem and see this thing that has happened, which the Lord has made known." (Luke 2 v 15)

I love this. *The Lord said it. Let's go see it.* It's just a complete wonderment at the glory and the involvement of God and an attitude of "I'm in." They are confident in what the God of glory has said, driving them to go see what God said would be waiting for them. They don't hold back. They go all in.

I want to be like that. In my Christian life, my faith can develop crusty edges. It becomes a routine. It becomes something that I talk about rather than do. But I want my life to be marked by saying, "The Lord said it; let's go see it." When I read how God says in the Bible that generosity changes the inner man and pleases him, I want to say, "The Lord said it; let's go see it." I want to get on with being generous, confident that what God has said will be waiting for me.

When I read in the Scriptures that God loves to call people to be forgiven and enjoy life with him, and that he uses his followers to share that news with those around them, I want there to bubble up in me confidence in what he says—I want that sense of adventure that says, "The Lord said it; let's go see it." I want to show people the God of glory, confident that he will work through me.

When I read about what God calls a husband to be—that he wants me to will love my wife like Christ loves the church, so that she will be like a well-watered vine that produces much fruit (metaphorically, not literally!)—I want to say, "The Lord said it; let's go see it." I want to work at being more and more that husband, confident that what God has said will be waiting for me.

"The Lord said it; let's go see it." That's an exciting and confident and purposeful way to live. When you see the glory of God, you get confident to go all in; you get that sense of adventure about your life—even on ordinary Tuesdays. The Lord said it; let's go see it.

KNOW YOU'RE LOVED

The glory of the Lord also came into the shepherds' lives that night. They saw this baby, who was God getting involved in his world. They heard that he had come not to condemn them and leave them outside, but to save them and beckon them in. What next?

They went back to shepherding:

> *The shepherds returned, glorifying and praising God for all they had heard and seen. (Luke 2 v 20)*

Nothing changed in the social standing of the shepherds. It's not as if all of a sudden, just because they had heard from angels and had gone to the manger and seen the Lord, their testimony would be admissible in a court of law. It's not as if all of a sudden they could hold office. It's not as if all of a sudden they were trusted in society's eyes.

Nothing like that changed or was fixed, yet they left rejoicing. The least likely people had found the most awesome joy.

Here's what the glory of God does. The glory of God injects gratitude and confidence into the highs and lows of our lives so that joy becomes the foundational emotion of life. If you let the glory of God expose you and if you hear that God has come to rescue and forgive you, you may not get your dream job or your dream marriage or your dream house… but you do get joy. You know that you're accepted. You know that you're loved. You know that God came for you and God is for you, regardless of whatever circumstances you're facing.

When the glory of God shows up, it changes everything. When you get a glimpse of the God of Christmas, things happen.

You get exposed.

You get afraid.

And then you find you don't need to feel that way. You're loved. And you know confidence and joy.

Forever.

God Is Worth It

I can pretty much guarantee that at some point during the Christmas season, you'll sing or hear these words:

Silent night, holy night.
All is calm, all is bright.

It's sweet, it's dainty, and it's not true. Of course it wasn't a silent night. A woman gave birth to her firstborn in an animal shed. I'm guessing there was some noise coming out of there. I'm betting it wasn't calm the whole way through.

Next, angels showed up, and a whole choir praised God out in the fields. Then, you had some shepherds charging into town and heading for the animal shed, before heading back out after a while, also praising God.

It wasn't a silent night, and we can't be silent about it today. If someone gave you this book, it's because they can't keep silent about it. It's because this was not just about a poor, illegitimate child being born in a manger. This was about a divine invasion, about the glory of God showing up… and this was an event that left the world utterly changed. And all this demands that you respond to it—one way or another.

See, Christmas tells us that Jesus is worth it. And by "it," I mean "everything." This God, who got involved to bring us joy, is worth our attention, our pursuit, and our trust.

WORTH YOUR ATTENTION

Christmas tells us that things can't be the same—that we can't stay put. It tells us to do what those famous "wise men" did:

> *Wise men from the east came to Jerusalem, saying, "Where is he who has been born king of the Jews? For we saw his star when it rose and have come to worship him." When Herod the king heard this, he was troubled, and all Jerusalem with him; and assembling all the chief priests and scribes of the people, he inquired of them where the Christ was to be born.*
>
> *They told him, "In Bethlehem of Judea, for so it is written by the prophet [God's messenger from seven centuries before, Micah]: 'And you, O Bethlehem, in*

the land of Judah, are by no means least among the rulers of Judah; for from you shall come a ruler who will shepherd my people Israel.'"

Then Herod ... sent them to Bethlehem ... They went on their way. And behold, the star that they had seen when it rose went before them until it came to rest over the place where the child was. When they saw the star, they rejoiced exceedingly with great joy. And going into the house, they saw the child with Mary his mother, and they fell down and worshiped him. Then, opening their treasures, they offered him gifts, gold and frankincense and myrrh.

And being warned in a dream not to return to Herod, they departed to their own country by another way.
(Matthew 2 v 1-12)

Let me tell you what we actually know about these "wise men from the east"...

They were wise men from the east. That's about it.

That's about all we know. They had obviously heard of some of the prophecies in the Old Testament—that one day God's King would be born among his people: the Jews. So when they "saw his star when it rose," they linked that new star to those prophecies. And then they did something. They began to move toward Jerusalem. They paid attention to what they had seen.

Paying attention to something is not the same thing as knowing something. Acting on something is not the same as understanding something.

And that's a problem when it comes to Christmas. Our problem is not that we don't know the story well enough. It's that we know the story too well. We know the details—angel, Bethlehem, no room at the inn, shepherds, angels, wise men, bad king… We know them so well that we fail to pay attention to them.

It's the same with Jesus himself. We know his stats. Laid in a manger, fed 5,000 guys with a packed lunch, walked on water, was kind to those on the edges of society, rode a donkey into the capital, got into trouble with the elites, died on a cross, and his tomb was found empty three days later. We know *about* him. But we don't *know* him.

DOING NOTHING

When that happens, we find ourselves in this story not with the wise men—seeing the star, packing up, and trekking west. We find ourselves in Jerusalem with the religious leaders—the chief priests and the scribes:

> [Herod] *inquired of them where the Christ was to be born. They told him, "In Bethlehem of Judea, for so it is written by the prophet: 'And you, O Bethlehem,*

in the land of Judah, are by no means least among the rulers of Judah; for from you shall come a ruler who will shepherd my people Israel.'" (Matthew 2 v 4-6)

They know the promise. They are the experts on the Christ, or Messiah—the promised all-powerful, divine King whom God promised to send. See how quickly they answer…

Herod: *Where is he going to be born?*

The religious guys: *Well, it's easy. The prophet says this: in Bethlehem of Judea.*

And then… nothing. Why didn't they start gathering their stuff and go? Why didn't they make a beeline for Bethlehem? Why weren't they searching the sky for the star?

They know about God's King. But they don't want to know him.

They know, but they pay no attention to what is going on just a few miles down the road from them.

Later, when he grew up, Jesus would put it bluntly to these guys:

You search the Scriptures because you think that in them you have eternal life; and it is they that bear witness about me, yet you refuse to come to me that you may have life. (John 5 v 39-40)

Their problem is not that they don't know the Bible. It's that they don't know Jesus. They miss the whole point of it.

Imagine, back when Lauren and I were dating, that I'd read a book about dating Lauren while I was out on a date with Lauren, and I'd read a chapter about how Lauren didn't like me reading books on dates—and then I hadn't put the book down.

Imagine me sitting there, thinking as I read, *Okay. Yeah. Useful stuff. Don't read when you're on a date. Where's my highlighter?*

Lauren: *Will you put that book down?*

Me: *Hey, do you mind? I'm trying to learn how to date you here.*

Here's the greatest challenge for us this Christmas. It's not making sure we have all the food cooked right, at the right time. It's not getting the right batteries for the toys we bought (not that anyone ever remembers to do this). It's not keeping everyone happy all day on the 25th. No—it's to pay attention to what was going on at the first Christmas. Not just knowing about Jesus, but knowing Jesus. A baby described as the Son of the Most High, God with us, the Lord, the Christ, and the Savior is worth our attention. If you're not sure who he is, the claims about him mean he's worth your consideration. He's worth you checking out whether he's true, and whether he's telling the truth.

And if you are sure of who he is, then let's not fall into the routine of doing the right religious stuff, knowing more about him but not drawing close to him. Going to church is not the same as seeing Jesus. Understanding theology is not the same as having your heart set on fire for him. Hear him in his word. Think about it. Pray to him about it. Count your blessings. See what he's calling you to. That takes time. And he's worth your time.

WORTH YOUR PURSUIT

Second, Jesus is worth your pursuit. These wise men really, really wanted to find this "king of the Jews." They wanted to meet him so much—here perhaps is the real Christmas miracle—that they stopped and asked for directions. What man does that?!

Why did these men do that? Travel so far. Put their plans on hold. Give so much time and energy and even admit they don't exactly know the way to the destination. Because they knew finding the King and knowing him was worth the pursuit. As Jesus described it himself once he grew up:

> *The kingdom of heaven is like treasure hidden in a field, which a man found and covered up. Then in his joy he goes and sells all that he has and buys that field.*
> *(Matthew 13 v 44)*

This man finds a treasure in the fields and then goes and joyfully sells everything he has. He loses everything he has to gain the field because he found treasure there. He's not giving up anything he won't gain back in many multiples. It's the best, most certain investment he will ever make.

The wise men were finding treasure because they were pursuing Jesus. Jesus is so excellent, so beautiful, that a loss of everything that gains us him should turn the loss of everything into joy. I'll gladly sell it all if I get him because there is nothing worth more than him.

Here's the fact: you have nothing you won't ultimately lose. Nothing! Let's be realistic. You're going to pack up your Christmas decorations one January and you won't get them out the next December because you won't be around. You'll have left them—and your house, and your family, and your work, and your investments— behind. Some of what you accumulated will go to a garage sale; some to landfill. Some will get handed down a few generations, but I'm guessing your great-great- grandchildren won't know your name (do you know *your* great-great-grandparents' names?)

Merry Christmas!

That sounds depressing. But it's not. It's OK—once you realize that it's different when it comes to Jesus. Get him and you never lose him. All of the lights are coming down, but he is not. All of the carols will go away, but people will still be praising his name in a million years. He is not going anywhere. He is the only one who, regardless of circumstances, regardless of life or death, doesn't move. He can't be moved.

That makes finding him and knowing him the only pursuit worth everything. Everyone has something that they pursue and are willing to give up anything else to get. But nothing else lasts and nothing else even satisfies.

If you are pursuing ultimate satisfaction in your relationship, I'm guessing it's starting to fracture under the burden of that demand. If you think work is going to satisfy you, I am guessing you are feeling restless or angry at work, or your life is a trainwreck. If you think people's approval of you is going to satisfy you, I'm betting you are feeling anxious and insecure, enslaved as you are to what others might be saying about you behind your back. And if none of that's true of you right now, it will be eventually.

Pursuing Jesus is different. He can handle the burden of our hopes and our dreams and our eternity. He came to give "life ... abundantly" (John 10 v 10). He came, as we've seen, to tell you that he knows everything about you and still loves you with everything he has. Investing your life in him is the only investment that yields dividends for eons. How do you know? Because his love is so great that he left heaven to come to earth to invite you into life with him. And because his power is so great that, at the other end of his life on earth, he rose from the grave to defeat death—the same death that mocks all your achievements and accumulations.

The wise men seemed to sense this. They sensed that this "king of the Jews" was worthy of their time, their money, and ultimately their eternity. He was worth pursuing—worth finding, and knowing.

And he still is.

WORTH YOUR EVERYTHING

Do you ever wonder what the wise men thought when they finally found Jesus—just this young child, aged two at most? What did they say to each other as they bowed down and worshiped him, and started to unpack the treasures they'd brought to give to him?

I don't know if you've been around two-year-olds. Most of them are cute, but I've never been around one who makes me want to worship them.

I wonder if those wise men were just looking over at each other, whispering…

Bill, I hate to bring this up again. But… this is a small child. In a little village. Are you sure about giving him your best thing? Is your wife going to be OK with you giving away that myrrh to this kid?

Well, Chuck, don't worry about my myrrh—you've just given him your gold.

Yeah, good point.

Surely they wondered, *We're here, we've found him, we have these possessions, and are we actually going to give them to him, or should we maybe just hang on to them?*

And we face the same choice. At Christmas, we come face to face with Jesus: God getting involved to expose us and to bring us forgiveness and joy.

Are we actually going to give what we have to him or hang on to it?

Let me put my cards on the table. I've been a Christian for 20 years, and I still struggle with this.

Here's how it works out for me. When it comes to 90 per cent of my life, I trust I can give it to Jesus and it'll be worth it. I trust him to work it out. But I have 10% I'm nervous about, which I want to hang on to. I cling to it instead of giving it up. Is Jesus worth me giving this up? Is Jesus worthy of my trust in handing over this thing?

I'm guessing you have those things, too. Maybe you sense that Jesus is the King. Maybe you say to others that Jesus is the King. But can you give your relationship hopes over to him? Your career plans? Your family's educational future? Your bank account? What's the 10%

that you want to hang on to as you stand and look this Christmas at the King in the manger?

The Bible tells us of a father who has a young son who is in the grip of evil (yes, the Bible says evil exists and demons are real forces. It helps you make sense of what you see all around you in the world if you believe there is such a thing as evil.) Can you imagine being that father? So he takes him to Jesus and essentially says, *My boy has seizures. He throws himself in the fire. We have no hope. Can you help?*

Jesus responds,

All things are possible for one who believes.

And this dad says:

I believe; help my unbelief! (Mark 9 v 24)

See what he's saying? *Jesus, I sense that you're good. I believe that you're powerful. I realize that you've come to drive out all that is broken, and bring healing and life eternal. But... I'm struggling to act on that. I'm struggling to give this over to you and trust you with it. I'm having a hard time living as though you are worth my trust, my everything. I believe. But please help me in my not-believing.*

And you know what? Jesus does. He heals the boy.

Jesus is worth your trust. He is worth giving everything to, including that 10% we all find hard. He can handle it.

The wise men grasped that. While the religious leaders were just hanging out in Jerusalem, reading about Jesus but missing out on knowing Jesus, the wise men got it. They gave Jesus their attention, their pursuit, and their trust. They gave him all they had, because they knew that he was worth it.

The Beginning, Not the End

I promised I'd tell you why I've relaxed my "not until Thanksgiving" rule about Christmas decorations.

Nine years ago, when I was 34, on Thanksgiving Day at the end of November, I had a seizure. That seizure revealed I had a tumor in my right frontal lobe. On December 4, I had a resection of the right frontal lobe. They cut a malignant oligodendroglioma out of my right frontal lobe.

I woke up from surgery with some weakness on my left side. I was released from rehab on December 16 with a gnarly scar on my head, and my hair starting to fall out, facing 18 months of high-dose chemo and radiation.

The first real outing I had was on Christmas Eve to come to Christmas Eve services at my church. As I sat at the back of the building, I could hardly hold it together.

It's hard to hold yourself together at Christmas when you've just heard the words, "You have a couple of years to live." It was a difficult Christmas for our family. I was wondering if it was going to be my last. They were wondering if it was going to be my last.

But it was OK.

It was OK because the brain tumor, which spoiled that Christmas and threatened to finish my life, didn't take away my hope. The beauty of the first Christmas is that God has got involved and put an anchor down for our souls, regardless of our circumstances.

And the beauty of Christmas is that it is just the start of the story—not the end. The story doesn't end with a baby in a manger or a man on a cross or even an empty tomb on a hillside.

The story hasn't ended. It ends on a day that has not yet come, when that baby, now a man and the Ruler of heaven, will return to this world and say, "Behold, I am making all things new" (Revelation 21 v 5).

That moment all of us are so hungry for—when everything is made right and perfect—is coming. But it's not going to be Christmas morning this year or next year or any year. It'll be at the return of the King of the universe. On that day, for those who know him now and who are looking forward to his coming, there will be the perfection we are all looking for. On that day, there will be no more depression, no more anxiety, no more loss, and no more brain tumors.

All that is sad, all that is dark, all that has gone wrong... there won't even be a remembrance of it. All that has been confusing, all of the moments we thought, "Where are you, God?" will vanish. Now, we live pressed up against a stained-glass window, and all we can see is bits of jagged glass. Then, we will be able to stand far enough back to see the beauty of it all.

And Christmas is the start of that story. Since that Christmas spent with "You have a couple of years to live" rolling round my mind, I've loved Christmas all the more. Christmas has got even better for me, because I've appreciated all the more that Christmas is when God got involved, gave me hope, and showed himself worthy of my trust. I love Christmas, all year round. And, yes, I love getting the decorations up way before December starts.

THE CHRISTMAS GIFT

Days after I sat up at the back of our church building that Christmas Eve, I started with the chemo and radiation. There were no guarantees of success. The side effects were often horrible. I prayed that God would help me keep knowing he was worth my trust. I prayed that God would help my family. I prayed that God would heal me. And, after nine months, the brain scans came back clear. After another couple rounds of chemo, I was given a clean bill of health. The tumor was gone.

The next November, Lauren's step-grandmother came for Thanksgiving, and she brought a Christmas present. So we had this one present sitting in our living room on the shelf for a month, waiting to be opened. Audrey was eight that year. And she'd just stare over at it. Even if the TV was on, she'd literally just be staring at the present. It was all she was looking forward to. There was this kind of giddy "I can't wait to open it" in her.

Well, two millennia ago, God came into his world. And he gave his world a present—himself. He came as a man: a man who lived and died and rose and who now reigns in heaven, and who will one day return and make everything perfect for all those who follow him. And if you accept this gift, you have everything to look forward to. You can always know your best days are ahead of you. Whatever else is going on in life, you can look at Jesus with a kind of giddy "I can't wait for him to come back" feeling.

Every December, the commercials promise us that perfection can be ours. But every Christmas, that perfection never truly comes—and it certainly never lasts. And yet perfection can be ours, forever—when Jesus comes again. So this season, you really can find all you want—not by looking to Christmas but beyond

Christmas, to the return of the one who came at that first Christmas.

That year I had the tumor, it snowed a ton at Christmas—the kind of real, legitimate, you-can-actu-ally-build-something-out-of-this snow that we almost never get in Texas. On Christmas Day, the kids were outside playing. I couldn't do anything because I'd just come out of brain surgery. You don't want to slip on the ice after that. All I could do was watch from inside, slightly dazed.

But here's what I can tell you. Jesus was enough. He was with me. He comforted me. He gave me joy. He gave me peace. He gave me hope.

And here's what else I can tell you. Having a brain tumor shows you what's important and what's worth celebrating. I relaxed the Chandler rule. We put the decorations up in November now. We watch *Elf* early.

I don't know what kind of year you've had and what kind of Christmas you're expecting as you read (or are looking back on as you read). Perhaps it's been truly a "joy to the world" kind of year for you. Perhaps your Christmas will be great. Remember that, for those who have welcomed Jesus into their life as King and asked him to invite them into his eternity, that's all just a shadow of what's coming when he returns. Praise God, enjoy Christmas… and look beyond it.

But maybe you're feeling beat up and banged up. Perhaps this is your first Christmas without a spouse. Or you're lonely. Or you can't get to where you'd like to be in life. Or you're struggling. Or you're sick or somebody you love is sick. Or something happened this year that has made you aware of how fragile things are. Remember— this is not all there is. God has got involved in the mess of this world so that he can share his joy with you now and bring you into his perfection one day. Invite him in, keep walking through the valleys and the peaks of this life with him… and look forward.

Christmas finishes, each year. What we look forward to soon lies behind us. But you can look forward to a day that will never end and a future that will never disappoint. The decorations get packed away, each year. But this year, hope and joy need not. You can look at the God who came and lay in that manger. And you can look forward to the day when he comes again.

And you can have an even better Christmas.

thegoodbook
COMPANY

BIBLICAL | RELEVANT | ACCESSIBLE

Thanks for reading this book. We hope you enjoyed it, and found it helpful.

Most people want to find answers to the big questions of life: Who are we? Why are we here? How should we live? But for many valid reasons we are often unable to find the time or the right space to think positively and carefully about them.

Perhaps you have questions that you need an answer for. Perhaps you have met Christians who have seemed unsympathetic or incomprehensible. Or maybe you are someone who has grown up believing, but need help to make things a little clearer.

At The Good Book Company, we're passionate about producing materials that help people of all ages and stages understand the heart of the Christian message, which is found in the pages of the Bible.

Whoever you are, and wherever you are at when it comes to these big questions, we hope we can help. As a publisher we want to help you look at the good book that is the Bible because we're convinced that as we meet the person who stands at its center—Jesus Christ—we find the clearest answers to our biggest questions.

Visit our website to discover the range of books, videos and other resources we produce, or visit our partner site christianityexplored.org for a clear explanation of who Jesus is and why he came.

Thanks again for reading,

Your friends at The Good Book Company

NORTH AMERICA thegoodbook.com 866 244 2165
UK & EUROPE thegoodbook.co.uk 0333 123 0880
AUSTRALIA thegoodbook.com.au (02) 9564 3555
NEW ZEALAND thegoodbook.co.nz (+64) 3 343 2463

 WWW.CHRISTIANITYEXPLORED.ORG
Our partner site is a great place for those exploring the Christian faith, with a clear explanation of the good news, powerful testimonies, and answers to difficult questions.